THE
DETROIT LIONS

Library of Congress Number: 81-70276   ISBN: 0-87191-811-0

Published by Creative Education, Inc., Mankato, Minnesota 56001

THE
DETROIT LIONS

JAMES R. ROTHAUS

CREATIVE EDUCATION, INC.
Mankato, Minnesota 56001

Detroit is known as the "Motor City." At the turn of the century, America's first automobile production lines opened in this southern Michigan city. Before long, the entire country depended on Detroit's cars for transportation.

Today, the people of Detroit have a lot of pride in their automobile industry. They also have a lot of pride in their sports teams. Football, baseball, basketball, hockey, soccer — Detroit has them all.

But there's a special place in the hearts of Detroit's sports fans for the Detroit Lions, their National Football League team. Because, like the city itself, the Lions have ruled the country. And, in harder times, they have struggled to keep up with their competition. But these Lions are no pussycats. They keep coming back, always aiming for the top and never satisfied once they get there. In that way, the Lions and the citizens of Detroit are a lot alike.

Following In Baseball's Footsteps

Considering Detroit's love of automobiles, you'd think its football team would be nicknamed the Motors, or the Limousines, or even the Jalopies. But back in

Earl "Dutch" Clark, the triple-threat star of Detroit's 1931 squad, could run, pass and kick. He came back in '37 and '38 to coach.

1934, Detroit's pro football team was named the Lions — because of baseball.

You see, George Richards, who paid $21,500 to bring the NFL team to Detroit from Portsmouth, Ohio, was also a radio station owner. So, naturally, he used his own station to conduct a "Name Your Team" contest.

Up to then, Detroit's major-league baseball team, the Tigers, had been the biggest show in town. And the fans thought that the football team should be as good as the baseball club. Hence, the Detroit Lions were born.

From the very start, Detroit fans had a lot to cheer about. The Lions won 10 games and lost just three that first year. Two of those losses were to the reigning powerhouse, the Chicago Bears, and their star, Bronko Nagurski.

Then, in 1935, the Lions won the Western Division title and advanced to the NFL championship game against the New York Giants. It seemed almost too good to be true when the Lions whalloped the Giants 26-7; Detroit had its first world championship!

In that game, Detroit's last touchdown was scored by rookie Raymond "Buddy" Parker — who would play a crucial role in the Lions' history almost 20 years later.

In 1940, halfback Byron "Whizzer" White ripped off 514 yards in rushing under Detroit coach Potsy Clark.

Here's a close look at Leon Hart, the Heisman trophy winner from Notre Dame, and the Lions' number one draft choice in 1950.

Detroit was 7-3 and third in the West in 1936. Then Earl "Dutch" Clark, a flashy, all-purpose tailback who starred for the team even before it moved to Detroit, took over the coaching duties. But Clark, who later became the first Detroit player elected to the Pro Football Hall of Fame, couldn't help what happened next. Age and injuries finally added up. And for the unlucky total of the next 13 seasons, the Lions won 55 games and lost 84. The fans in Detroit still loved their team, but they knew the Lions needed some help. That's exactly what they got, smack dab in the middle of the 20th century.

High Hopes for the '50's

Edwin J. Anderson, president of the Lions, announced that 1950 would be "the make or break year," the year of decision. The decisions, it turned out, would make the Lions champions again.

Four key people joined the team that year:

First was Bobby Layne, a rangy quarterback from Santa Anna, Texas, who was tall, blond, tousle-haired, and a little on the chunky side. Bobby was easy to spot on the field — he was the player wearing cardboard-thin shoulder pads and no hip pads at all. But if there was one thing that Bobby Layne did well, it was throw the football.

Second was Ewell Doak Walker, Jr., a little halfback from Dallas, Texas. He liked to be called just plain old "Doak". He and Layne had played together at Highland Park High School, and Walker could run with the pigskin as well as Layne could pass it. Walker was only 5-foot-11 and 170 pounds, but he had an uncanny ability to dash towards the sidelines, put on the brakes to let a defender fly by, and then move back into high gear and race towards the goalline.

Third was Leon Hart, who was as big as Walker was small. As a senior at Notre Dame, Hart became the second lineman in history to win the famous Heisman Trophy. At Detroit, he balanced Walker's quickness and Layne's finesse with pure and simple muscle.

The fourth key person who came to Detroit in 1950 was Buddy Parker — although the owners, players and fans may not have realized right then how important he was to be. Yes, this is the same Buddy Parker who scored the final touchdown in the Lions' title game in 1935. He became an assistant coach in 1950. After the Lions went 6-6 that season, he moved up to head coach.

The cornerstones were set; a dynasty was about to be built.

Doak goes for broke. Detroit's 1950 team saw sensational rookie Ewell "Doak" Walker become NFL scoring champ with 128 points.

Detroit Hall of Famer, Bobby Layne, drove the team to two straight NFL champion-
ships in '52 and '53.

The Motor City fans had a feeling that Layne, Walker, Hart and the other new Detroit players just might start something special. Attendance doubled at old Briggs Stadium, and the Lions finished the '51 season 7-4-1, right behind the mighty Los Angeles Rams.

Hopes were high for 1952, but the Lions lost to the San Francisco 49'ers in the season-opener. They barely beat the Rams, but the 49'ers came back and clobbered them again. A lesser team might have let down, but not these Lions. They would not quit.

Instead, they watched and learned from Walker, who forgot that he was inches shorter and pounds lighter than every other player on the field. He darted, stopped, juked and sped his way toward the endzone. In his own quiet way, he inspired his teammates.

They heard Layne who, in his unusual high-pitched voice, urged all of them to give 110 percent in each and every practice. Bobby, who could criticize a player one minute and joke with him the next, told his teammates with a smile, "I've never lost a ball game . . . but sometimes time has run out on me."

And so they began to win. Detroit outscored its opponents in six of its next seven games, and finished the regular season with a 9-3 record. The Lions then demolished the Rams for the third time that year to advance to the championship game against Cleveland.

The score was tied 7-7 in that game when Doak Walker trotted onto the field in the middle of the second quarter. He had been injured much of the season, but the fans in Cleveland knew that Walker often performed his best under the toughest conditions. They held their breath.

Doak bent over the Detroit huddle and heard his name called for the next play. He took his position behind the line of scrimmage. The ball was snapped and the pitch came his way. Walker grabbed the ball, tucked it into the crook of his right arm, and popped through the middle of the Cleveland line. Suddenly, a Browns linebacker appeared, waiting to wrap Walker up for no gain. "The Doaker" didn't even flinch. He planted his right foot and made a cut that propelled him about six feet to his left. The linebacker, frozen in his tracks, could only watch as the little Lion turned on the speed and roared 67 yards for a touchdown. Detroit won the game, 17-7, and was back on top of the National Football League.

Joe Schmidt, Detroit's legendary teeth-rattling linebacker, made defensive history in the late 50's and early 60's.

Dick "Night Train" Lane rolled into Detroit in 1960, adding even more muscle to the crunching Lions' defense.

"Honeymooning" in Detroit

A new football coach usually has what sportswriters call "a honeymoon" — that magical period of time when everyone is solidly behind him. For most coaches, the honeymoon lasts only a game or two; lucky ones have a whole year of it. But Buddy Parker's honeymoon with the Lions lasted almost three whole years.

The 1953 season was practically a Xerox copy of the previous year. In the championship game, against Cleveland, the Lions were behind 16-10 with the clock ticking down. But Bobby Layne remembered his motto. He wouldn't let time run out on him. He passed short . . . he passed long . . . he ran the ball downfield . . . and the Lions scored to tie the game at 16.

The Detroit crowd went wild as Doak Walker lined up for the point-after attempt. The noise died down, and for an instant, the only sound was that of Walker's foot soundly booting the ball upward. There wasn't a moment's doubt — the ball sailed between the uprights and the crown was Detroit's once more.

It looked like the NFL title would stay in the Motor City for a third straight year when the Lions won the division championship one year later, but Cleveland finally beat the jinx in 1954. Actually, the Browns' Otto Graham did most of the damage to Detroit, as he ran for three touchdowns, passed for three more, and led Cleveland to a lopsided, 56-10 win.

Detroit fans would like to forget the 1955 season, when the Lions were 3-9 and finished last in the Western Division. But the next year, they rebounded for second behind Chicago, and in 1957 the Lions again met Cleveland for the world championship.

But Detroit was missing two people who had meant so much to its earlier wins. First, Coach Buddy Parker had resigned before the first pre-season game. And second, Bobby Layne had a broken leg.

It looked bleak for the Lions. Who would replace Layne?

Backup signal-caller Tobin Rote knew he wasn't another Bobby Layne. He was simply a solid number-two quarterback who had just come to Detroit in a trade with Green Bay early that season.

But Rote had made good use of the time he had spent on the bench when Layne wasn't hurt. He had memorized the plays, watched the receivers run their patterns, and kept his own running and passing skills in game-ready shape.

High-stepping Lem Barney was the league's defensive rookie of the year in '67 . . . but the Lions finished 5-7-2.

Big, fast Alex Karras played a fearsome tackling role for the Detroit teams of the 60s.

More than 55,000 fans, many of whom had stood in line for hours to get tickets, watched nervously as Rote jogged onto Briggs Field.

But it took only moments for the rest of the Lions to realize that Tobin Rote *could* replace Layne — at least right then. Rote threw four touchdown passes and ran the ball over the goalline once himself. And before the Browns knew what hit them, the Lions had won, 59-14, for their third championship in six years.

Tough Times In Detroit

There's another word sportswriters use in football; this one refers to a team that always finishes second. They call that team "the bridesmaid", the runner-up, the squad that didn't quite make it to the top.

Well, that's what happened to the Lions during the next 22 seasons. From 1956 to 1978, Detroit was second in its division 12 times; once the Lions were number two for seven straight seasons!

Now for many teams, second place would be just fine, thank you. After all, there are plenty of third-, fourth- and fifth-place teams that would love to hold down that second-place slot. But the Lions had tasted the sweetness of being champions, and they weren't satisfied with just trying harder to be number two.

While Detroit couldn't quite make it to the top, the players and coaches did show the rest of the NFL a thing or two about defense. They practiced their pass rush; they drilled on stopping a running game; they worked extra hours to be good enough to stop any offense thrown at them.

It wasn't long before Detroit had the reputation throughout the league as being one of the toughest defensive teams around. Bobby Layne had been traded; Doak Walker retired. But in 1958, the already-awesome defense got another boost from burly Alex Karras, a rookie draft choice from the University of Iowa.

Karras was his name, and tackling was his game. Actually, Karras was so nearsighted that he could hardly see the scoreboard. He wore big, thick glasses off the field, but no one dared laugh at this 6-foot-2, 250-pound defensive tackle. He was so quick that he could plug holes faster than any offensive line could create them. Play after play, game after game, running backs tested Karras' side of the line. And play after play, game after

Down he goes. Ace quarterback Greg Landry put lots of points on the board during the "frustrating 70's."

The Detroit fans liked Landry's tousle-haired looks. But they liked his passing arm even better.

game, few players passed that test and graduated into the open field.

When a runner happened to get by Karras, he'd run headlong into Joe Schmidt. Schmidt came to the Lions in 1953 from the University of Pittsburgh. And throughout his career, when he wasn't bringing down running backs, he'd be "red dogging," that sudden defensive rush into the offensive backfield that kept quarterbacks looking nervously over their shoulders.

The Turkey Day Massacre

Thanksgiving Day, 1962, was what the Detroit defense was all about. To this day, it's still called "The Turkey Day Massacre." Here's what happened:

The Green Bay Packers came to Detroit brimming with confidence, and rightly so. They were undefeated after 10 games, and they led the league in most statistical categories. Bart Starr was at the controls, and he was also at the top of the NFL's list for passing.

Detroit was 7-2, a pretty good record in itself. But everyone knew the Lions didn't have a chance.

Everyone, that is, except the proud Detroit defense.

Joe Schmidt warned the fans the day before the game: "We'll beat the Packers this time." No one listened.

Detroit's task was not simple. The defense had to stop Starr's pinpoint passing. That required spreading out the linebackers and defensive backs. But they also had to worry about running back Jim Taylor, who could plow right through a weakened defensive line. Experts knew that the Packers would find Detroit's defensive weakness; the only questions seemed to be, when and where?

Detroit kicked off to start the game. Starr walked up to the line of scrimmage on Green Bay's first possession. Facing him were Darris McCord, Karras, Roger Brown and Sam Williams — Detroit's "Fearsome Foursome."

Behind them were linebackers Schmidt, Wayne Walker and Carl Bennett. The Green Bay quarterback had seen them all before. But this time, what was that glow in their eyes?

Starr found out soon enough. The Lion defense was "psyched" — about as high as it could be. Three times the Packers tried the line; three times they were stopped cold.

Detroit scored first, after its defense forced a short Green Bay punt. Following the kickoff, the Packers were again stopped for no gain. Starr was feeling the pressure now. "Keep those guys off me, eh?" he told his team-

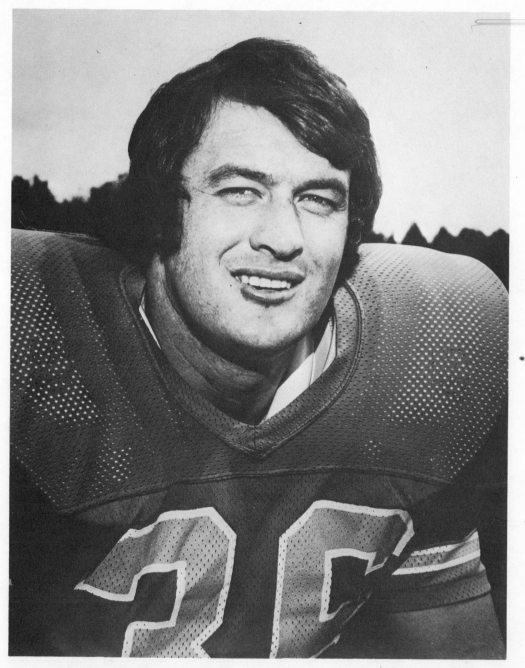

Running back Steve Owens had plenty to smile about after the '74 Lions came back to win seven of their last 10 games.

mates in the huddle. But it was too late; the tempo of the game was set.

The Fearsome Foursome were playing frenzied ball. They brushed aside Packer offensive linemen as if they were styrofoam dummies. Time and time again, they forced Starr for losses as he attempted to pass. Jim Taylor crashed into the Lions' forward wall with such little success that he must have thought the wall was made of granite blocks. The Packer offense was helpless.

The Detroit defense forced a fumble, leading to another touchdown; now it was 14-0. Then Karras, Williams and McCord all smashed into Starr at the same time as the Green Bay field general was looking to pass. The ball popped into the air . . . Williams scooped it up . . . and ran it into the endzone for the third Lion TD. Less than one minute later, the onrushing defense caught Starr in the endzone for a safety, and the score rose to 23-0.

The Lions wouldn't let up. They even tried a 47-yard field goal — and it was good! Vince Lombardi, the celebrated coach of the Packers, paced up and down the sidelines. Who were those Detroit defenders out there? What could stop them? Time was running out, and all

Thanksgiving Day, 1976. The Lions' Charlie Sanders (88) draws a bead on a Buffalo running back.

Green Bay could manage was two trips into the end-zone. It wasn't enough. The final score read Lions 26, Packers 14. The Turkey Day Massacre was complete.

In the Detroit locker room, the players seemed stunned at their own inspired performance. They had no real explanations ready for the press, just those half-exhausted, half-exhilarated grins on their faces. Even Coach George Wilson was momentarily speechless. Finally, he took a deep breath, and spoke:

"Well, fellows," he said with a sigh, and a little smile began to creep across his face, "have a happy Thanksgiving!"

Bill Ford Takes Over

While the Detroit defense was making headlines, the Lions changed owners for the fourth time since 1934. In 1964, William Clay Ford bought the Lions for $6.5 million. (That's $6,478,500 more than what George Richards paid for the team just 30 years earlier.)

Ford was the grandson of Henry Ford, the famous car manufacturer who opened one of the first automobile plants in Detroit in the early 1900's. And William Clay Ford was an owner who loved his team as much as the rest of Detroit did — and maybe more.

It took three Bengals to bring down fleet-footed Lion Dexter Bussey in this 1977 pre-season contest.

Quarterback Gary Danielson strings one out against the 1978 San Diego Chargers.

Way back in 1934, Edsel Ford had taken his young son Bill to see the "new" football team that had just moved to the Motor City from Portsmouth, Ohio. Bill Ford liked what he saw. Little did he know that he'd one day own that same team.

In the seasons that passed after Ford bought the Lions, players came and went, many good, some great. Fans loved Greg Landry, the quarterback who liked to run almost as much — and maybe just a little bit more — as he liked to pass. They idolized Lem Barney, the cornerback who dominated the special teams for kick returns, and who kept his corner of the field on defense free of completed passes. And they watched Earl "The Pearl" McCullouch with joy as the former world-class hurdler sprinted the sidelines to make diving, twisting, game-breaking receptions.

Still, it seemed that the "right" combination of players was never quite there. Even when the Lions moved from Briggs Field into a new stadium in 1975, the bridesmaid streak continued.

The new facility was located in Pontiac, Michigan. Unlike the concrete-domed stadiums, this building was topped with an inflatable, fiberglass roof. At first it was named Pontiac Metropolitan Stadium, or "Ponmet" for short. But that name didn't have a big-league ring to it, so next year, it was changed to the Pontiac Silverdome.

Wouldn't you know it? Even the stadium's name gave the feeling of second place. After all, gold medals are awarded for first place, and silver ones mean second.

To add insult to injury, the long string of second- and third-place finishes was followed, in 1979, with a 2-14 record. The last time the Lions had won only two games was in 1948. Once again, the fans were hoping for that one great player who could turn this team around. And again, that's just what they got.

Billy Sims Brings New Roar To The Lions

His name is Billy Sims. He was all-everything at the University of Oklahoma. He won the Heisman Trophy when he was just a junior. He was the very first pick of the 1980 draft of college players. He had a big salary, a big reputation, and plenty of big expectations to live up to when he came to town.

So what did Billy Sims do?

He drove into Detroit in a Chevrolet pickup truck, to

Ken Fantetti (57) held on to make the tackle when the Lions met the Bears in a '79 mini-war at the Pontiac Silverdome.

No you don't. James Hunter (28) shut down a Chicago drive in mid-season 1980.

go to work for William Clay Ford, whose family, you may remember, makes a rival brand of cars.

He signed a three-year contract for $1.7 million. That was fine for Sims, but many veteran Detroit players were a little uncertain that this untested rookie could be worth more than four or five of them put together.

So Billy Sims stood up in front of the veteran players one day at the training camp dinner and introduced himself, as all rookies must do:

"I'm Billy Sims from Oklahoma," he said in his slight drawl, as the players around him wondered if this hot-shot, high-paid upstart would really fit into the team. "And I'm the reason you guys didn't get raises this year."

That did it. Even the biggest, baddest defensive linemen had to laugh. Billy was one of them.

And, finally, Billy Sims helped take a last-place football team and get it steamrolling through the NFL.

September 7, 1980, Detroit opened its season against the Los Angeles Rams in Anaheim, California. Sims, who had caught only two passes in his entire *career* at Oklahoma, ran a crossing pattern through the Rams defense. Bob Brudzinski, the L.A. linebacker, stumbled a little as he moved toward the rookie running back. By the time Brudzinski looked up, Sims had the ball and was 15 yards downfield. Johnnie Johnson, the Rams' million-dollar rookie, could only wave as Sims high-tailed it past him. A normal 10-yard gain became a 60-yard touchdown. Detroit won the game, 41-20.

September 14, 1980. Detroit flew into Green Bay to meet the Packers. The Lions hadn't won here in five years — but Billy Sims didn't know that. He took a handoff, and — whoops! — his hole disappeared. No problem. Sims lowered his body slightly . . . bounced to the left with his massive thighs supplying the power . . . ran over a couple of would-be tacklers — and turned a one-yard loss into a 25-yard gain. Detroit won again, 29-7.

That was two wins in two games — it had taken the Lions all of 1979 to win two games! And Sims had four TDs — no one in Detroit had scored more than five during all of the previous season.

On and on went the Billy Sims Lions. The people of Detroit loved their rookie sensation — he took what he was given, which usually was just a yard or two, and he made it into something exciting, like a slashing run, a

One more for Freddy. The Lions' Fred Scott drove the Cardinals crazy in this early 1980 contest.

diving catch, or one of his patented, side-stepping trips into the end zone.

Still, Sims didn't have to do it all on his own. As if by magic, that "right" combination was suddenly there.

Quarterback Gary Danielson gritted his teeth and came back from a knee injury to pass for a record 3,223 yards. He threw only 11 interceptions all year, the lowest total in the conference.

Veteran running back Dexter Bussey unselfishly moved to fullback to make room for Sims, and wound up rushing for 720 yards himself. That put him second on the Lions' all-time leading rushing chart.

The Detroit defense lived up to the tradition of stingy Lion stop-squads. Opposing running backs started to dread the day they'd have to try to punch through the league's top defense against the run.

And, of course, there was Sims, who ran for a record 1,303 yards, shattered four other Detroit marks, and was everybody's Rookie of the Year.

Behind these great players was Head Coach Monte Clark. Owner Bill Ford hired Clark in 1978, and for two years, the 6-foot-6 Clark watched his Lions win nine

Hard-hitting Charlie Weaver looks for a Lion championship in '81 or '82.

games and lose 23. He was discouraged, but that discouragement only made him more determined to succeed.

Clark never dreamed up wild excuses for the losses. He was patient with the press and the public, some of whom could still remember that last championship season in 1957. And he never criticized his players in public. In two years, while Monte Clark was earning the respect of players and fans alike, he was quietly building the cornerstones of a solid football team.

Sound familiar? Just like the 1950 Lions, today's team has those all-important "key people." In 1950, the quarterback was Layne; in 1980, it was Danielson. The memory of Doak Walker is being rivaled by Billy Sims. Buddy Parker's coaching wizardry led Detroit 30 years earlier; now Monte Clark can fill those shoes.

The Lions are ready to roar again.

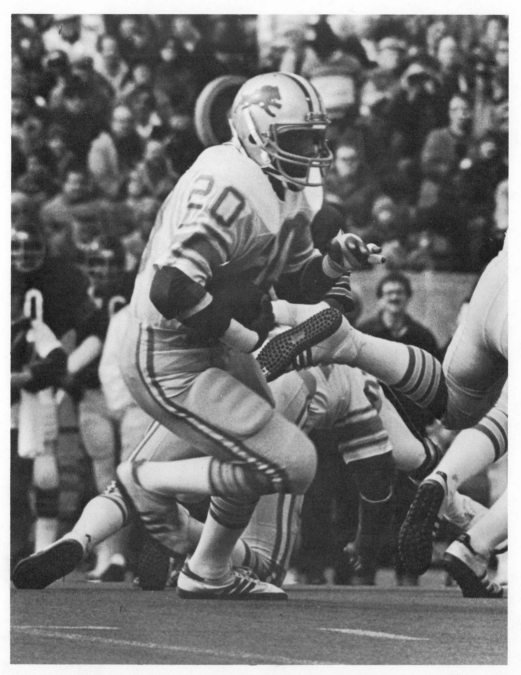

The pride 'n joy of the Lions backfield, Billy Sims, heads for daylight against the 1980 Bears.

Billy Sims hits paydirt. He'll be tough to stop as the Lions seek more glory in the 80's.

The Detroit Lions entered the National Football League in 1934 when the Portsmouth Spartans moved to the Motor City. The Lions competed in the Western Division of the NFL until 1968. Then, for two years, they were members of the Central Division of the Western Conference. When the NFL and the American Football League merged in 1970, the Lions became part of the Central Division of the National Football Conference, where they still compete today.

Year	Won	Lost	Tied	Pct.
Portsmouth Spartans				
1930	5	6	3	.909
1931	11	3	0	.786
1932	6	2	4	.750
1933	6	5	0	.545
Detroit Lions				
1934	10	3	1	.769
1935	7	3	2	.700
1936	8	4	0	.667
1937	7	4	0	.636
1938	7	4	0	.636
1939	6	5	0	.545
1940	5	5	1	.500
1941	4	6	1	.400
1942	0	11	0	.000
1943	3	6	1	.333
1944	6	3	1	.667
1945	7	3	0	.700
1946	1	10	0	.091
1947	3	9	0	.250
1948	2	10	0	.167
1949	4	8	0	.333
1950	6	6	0	.500
1951	7	4	1	.636
1952	9	3	0	.750
1953	10	2	0	.833
1954	9	2	1	.818
1955	3	9	0	.250
1956	9	3	0	.750
1957	8	4	0	.667
1958	4	7	1	.364
1959	3	8	1	.273
1960	7	5	0	.583
1961	8	5	1	.615
1962	11	3	0	.786

1963	5	8	1	.385
1964	7	5	2	.583
1965	6	7	1	.462
1966	4	9	1	.308
1967	5	7	2	.417
1968	4	8	2	.333
1969	9	4	1	.692
1970	10	4	0	.714
1971	7	6	1	.538
1972	8	5	1	.607
1973	6	7	1	.464
1974	7	7	0	.500
1975	7	7	0	.500
1976	6	8	0	.429
1977	6	8	0	.429
1978	7	9	0	.438
1979	2	14	0	.125
1980	9	7	0	.563

COACHES

1930-36	George (Potsy) Clark	53-26-10
1937-38	Earl (Dutch) Clark	14- 8- 0
1939	Elmer (Gus) Henderson	6- 5- 0
1940	George (Potsy) Clark	5- 5- 1
1941-42	Bill Edwards*	4- 9- 1
1942	John Karcis	0- 8- 0
1943-47	Gus Dorais	20-31- 2
1948-50	Alvin (Bo) McMillin	12-24- 0
1951-56	Raymond (Buddy) Parker	47-23- 2
1957-64	George Wilson	53-45- 6
1965-66	Harry Gilmer	10-16- 2
1967-72	Joe Schmidt	43-34- 7
1973	Don McCafferty	6- 7- 1
1974-76	Rick Forzano**	15-17- 0
1976-77	Tommy Hudspeth	5- 5- 0
1978	Monte Clark	18-30- 0

*Replaced after three games in 1942
**Resigned after four games in 1976